R.E.A.D. Dogs

by Meish Goldish

Consultant: Kathy Klotz, Executive Director
Intermountain Therapy Animals/
Reading Education Assistance Dogs® (R.E.A.D.®)

New York, New York

Credits

COV, © Tina Anderson; TOC, © Tina Anderson; 4, © matsou/iStockphoto; 5, © Barbara Babikian & Kaila; 6, © Barbara Babikian & Kaila; 7, © Barbara Babikian & Kaila; 8, © Todd Bennett/Staff/ ZUMA Press/Newscom; 9, © Marmaduke St. John/Alamy; 10, © Andrew Knapp/Find MoMo/ Quirk; 11, © ZUMA Press, Inc / Alamy; 12, © courtesy of Longview News Journal; 13, © courtesy of Longview News Journal; 14, © Patti Shanaberg, Angel Paw, Pet Partners & R.E.A.D. registered Therapy Team, Angel Paws; 15, © courtesy of Nancy Brooks, R.E.A.D. Dogs MN; 16, © AP Photo/Manuel Balce Ceneta; 17, © Tina Anderson; 17B, © Tina Anderson; 18, © Todd Bennett/Staff/ZUMA Press/ Newscom; 19L, © Byelikova Oksana/Shutterstock; 19R, © jamesbenet/iStockphoto; 20, © Cody Neff/ The Register-Herald; 21, © Jamie Jones for Reading Education Assistance Dogs; 22, © Patti Shanaberg, Angel Paw, Pet Partners & R.E.A.D. registered Therapy Team, Angel Paws; 22B, © AP Photo/ The Journal Times, Gregory Shaver; 23, © Tina Anderson; 24, © Wags for Hope; 25, © AP Photo/ Douglas Bovitt; 26, © AP Photo/The Express-Times, Stephen Flood; 27, © Tina Anderson; 28, © Tina Anderson.

R.E.A.D. and Reading Education Assistance Dogs are registered trademarks belonging to Intermountain Therapy Animals.

Publisher: Kenn Goin
Editor: Jessica Rudolph
Creative Director: Spencer Brinker
Design: Dawn Beard Creative
Photo Researcher: We Research Pictures, LLC

Library of Congress Cataloging-in-Publication Data

Goldish, Meish, author.
  R.E.A.D. dogs / by Meish Goldish.
    pages cm. — (Dog heroes)
  Includes bibliographical references and index.
  ISBN 978-1-62724-517-3 (library binding) — ISBN 1-62724-517-0 (library binding)
  1. Working dogs—Juvenile literature. 2. Dogs—Therapeutic use—Juvenile literature. 3. Learning disabled children—Education—Juvenile literature. I. Title. II. Title: READ dogs. III. Series: Dog heroes.
  SF428.2.G657 2015
  636.7088—dc23
                            2014034556

For more information, write to Bearport Publishing Company, Inc., 45 West 21st Street, Suite 3B, New York, New York 10010. Printed in the United States of America.

10 9 8 7 6 5 4 3 2 1

Table of Contents

A Furry Helper

When twelve-year-old Hannah Castine was in first grade, she hated to read. "I was not a very good reader," she explains. "I really couldn't read at all." Hannah has **dyslexia**. A few years ago, it was very difficult for her to recognize letters and words on a page. She also had trouble **pronouncing** words. As a result, Hannah refused to read aloud in front of her classmates.

Some people with dyslexia see letters backwards or upside down. Others see letters that look bunched together or out of order. For some, words seem to move around on the page.

The word *dyslexia* shown on top is upside down. This is how some readers with dyslexia see words on a page.

Luckily, Hannah soon met someone at school who helped her improve her reading skills. Hannah's partner was Kaila—a Shetland sheepdog! Dogs can't read. So how was the **canine** able to help Hannah?

Over the years, Kaila has helped many kids become better readers.

The Perfect Partner

Kaila the sheepdog helped Hannah read better simply by being a good listener. Every week, Hannah spent 15 minutes in a quiet area of her school reading aloud to Kaila. The dog snuggled with the young girl as she read. Hannah was happy. She remembers thinking, "Wow, someone understands and cares about what I'm reading."

Kaila looks at a book as a young student reads to her.

While reading to Kaila, Hannah felt relaxed, even when she mispronounced a word. She wasn't nervous or embarrassed, as she was with her classmates. When Hannah read aloud to Kaila, the dog's owner, Barbara Babikian, sat with them. She helped Hannah pronounce hard words and explained their meanings. After many months, Hannah was reading faster and with greater **confidence**. She says, "Kaila helped me a lot. She made reading a lot more fun and easier."

Kaila with her owner, Barbara Babikian

Many teachers think dogs are the perfect partners for struggling readers. The animals never laugh at children or make fun of them for not knowing a word or saying it wrong.

A New Idea

Before she met Hannah, Kaila worked as a **therapy dog**. Her owner Barbara brought her Shetland sheepdog to nursing homes to visit **residents** there. Later, she wanted to find a way for Kaila to help children, too. Barbara heard about a program called R.E.A.D., which stands for Reading Education Assistance Dogs.

A therapy dog named Brooks plays with a nursing home resident.

Many therapy dogs go to hospitals and nursing homes to visit people wh are sick or **depressed**. People are encouraged to pet the animals, which can help them relax and feel better.

The R.E.A.D. program was the idea of Sandi Martin. As a nurse working in Utah, she saw how therapy dogs cheered up hospital patients. Sandi knew that kids who read poorly are often unhappy and nervous in the classroom. She wondered: Could therapy dogs help struggling readers just like they help sick people?

A snuggle from a therapy dog can lift a patient's spirits.

Starting at the Library

In 1999, Sandi helped create the first R.E.A.D. program at a library in Salt Lake City, Utah. Children of all reading abilities were allowed to sign up. Each child read to a dog once a week for four weeks. Kids who came at least three times were rewarded with a new book, which was "pawtographed" by their dog partner.

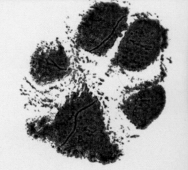

A "pawtograph" is a dog's paw print made with ink.

HI THERE!

I'm Andrew, and this is my buddy Momo.

He likes to hide. In fact, Momo's hiding in every picture in this book.

Think you can

The R.E.A.D. program was organized by Intermountain Therapy Animals (ITA), which is based in Salt Lake City. The group provides therapy animals to people in need. Sandi Martin is a member of ITA.

As Sandi Martin had hoped, the library **experiment** was a big hit. Youngsters felt at ease with their dog partners right away. As a result, more R.E.A.D. programs were set up in libraries in other cities in Utah, as well as in other states and countries.

In some libraries, children who are too young to read can still take part in R.E.A.D. programs. The dog's owner reads aloud to the child and the dog.

Class Canines

As the R.E.A.D. program spread to more places, dog owners brought their canines to schools as well. When a dog works in a school, not all students in a classroom take part. Instead, teachers or reading **specialists** pick the children they feel need the most help and will gain the most from the program.

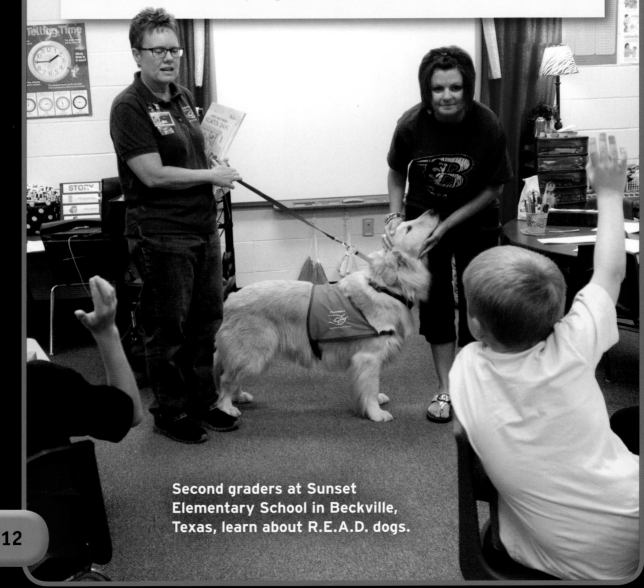

Second graders at Sunset Elementary School in Beckville, Texas, learn about R.E.A.D. dogs.

Elvis, a golden retriever, is a popular guest at Sunset Elementary School. Students who read to him always look forward to his visits. Sue Ogden, a first-grade teacher, says, "Elvis gives them a chance to feel good about themselves and about reading. They consider it a special treat to be allowed to spend time reading with him."

Some R.E.A.D. dogs, like Elvis, wear capes or vests to let people know they are working.

Growing Close

In most schools, students meet with their R.E.A.D. dogs once a week. As the weeks go on, the children and dogs start to feel very comfortable together. During a **session**, a student-dog pair sits in a quiet part of the classroom with the dog's owner, away from other students. The child can play with the dog for the first few minutes. Then reading begins.

Students and their dog partners often become good friends!

Each R.E.A.D. session can last up to 30 minutes.

Many students like to pet their dogs while reading. This helps the children relax. Often, dogs rest their heads on readers' laps. Some dogs are even trained to turn book pages with their noses or paws. After reading time ends, children can spend a few minutes giving treats to their reading partners.

Many dogs like to rest their heads on students.

Who's the Student?

When a child reads aloud to a dog, the dog's owner or **handler** plays an important part. Colleen Foti owns a R.E.A.D. dog named Toby. If a child stumbles on a hard word, Colleen will help by pronouncing it. Then she'll say something like, "Toby has never heard the word *hooves* before. Andrew, can you tell him what it means?"

Barbara (right) is this dog's handler. She helps a student with difficult words.

R.E.A.D. dog owners and handlers are trained to always speak as if the dog is also being taught, not just the child. That way, the child is less likely to feel embarrassed for not knowing a word.

If the child doesn't know the answer, Colleen opens a dictionary. Together, they look up the word. Then Colleen explains its meaning while speaking to the dog. She'll say, "Toby, *hooves* means a horse's feet." She may pretend the dog has said something. Colleen will then say to the student, "Wow, Toby thinks that is a great word!"

This collie named Roo helps lots of kids. Roo often looks like he's the one being taught to read.

Becoming a Therapy Dog

The R.E.A.D. program is always looking for more dogs to help young readers in schools and libraries. However, not just any canine can take part. All R.E.A.D. dogs must first be tested and **registered** as therapy dogs. During the tests, they have to show that they can obey all basic **commands**, such as "sit" and "stay." The dogs must also remain quiet and gentle, even in **stressful** situations.

A therapy dog must always be calm, even when it sees things that are strange or new, such as a wheelchair.

Carol Vickers describes a test that her chocolate Labrador retriever, Summerlee, had to pass at a hospital to become a therapy dog. "They brought out people in hospital gowns with **walkers** and wheelchairs to see how she would react. They threw things and made loud noises." Summerlee stayed calm and didn't panic or bark. "She passed!" says Carol.

Before seeing patients in a hospital, therapy dogs are washed with shampoo to clean off dirt and kill **fleas**. The shampoo also gives the animals a pleasant smell.

Training for R.E.A.D.

After Summerlee became a therapy dog, she needed even more training to **qualify** as a R.E.A.D. dog. She had to be able to sit quietly for half an hour. She also had to learn to look at a book and pay attention as someone read aloud from it.

Carol Vickers reads to Summerlee to get her used to listening to students.

To train her dog, Carol first laid a quilt on the floor at her home and placed a book on the quilt. She put dog treats between the book's pages. Carol would then say "Look" and start reading from the book. The smell and taste of the treats made Summerlee look at the book's pages. Over time, Summerlee learned to look and listen even when no treats were given.

To become a R.E.A.D. dog, a canine must be able to stay quiet when children in a classroom move around and make noise. A dog should never jump on a person, bark, bite, or growl—even if a child is pulling on its fur.

R.E.A.D. dogs are trained to listen as well as look when a child reads.

It Takes All Kinds

Any kind of dog that passes all its tests can join the R.E.A.D. program. R.E.A.D. dogs come in all **breeds** and sizes—from tiny terriers to giant mastiffs. Some children like small dogs that can curl up in their laps as they read. Other kids prefer big dogs to gently lean against.

The R.E.A.D. program tries to give children a choice in picking the kind of dog they would like as a partner—big or small.

This huge R.E.A.D. dog is a mastiff.

Some children, however, are not comfortable around dogs. For these students, the R.E.A.D. program uses other kinds of animals, including cats, bunnies, and guinea pigs. Kids can even read to an African Grey parrot.

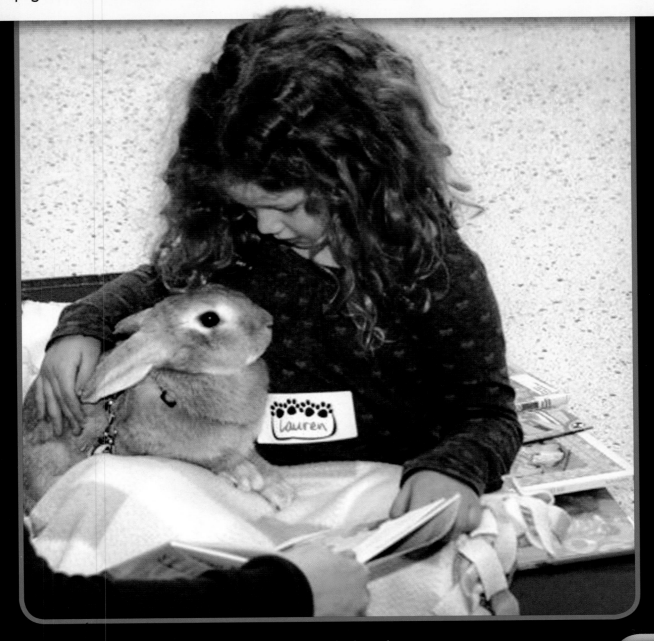

A student reads to a bunny.

Having a Bad Day

Even with all its training, a R.E.A.D. dog may have a bad day once in a while. Sometimes a dog is **restless** and wants to move around during the session. The owner may take the animal for a bathroom break or offer it a drink of water before having the child continue reading.

A dog's owner or handler is always there to make sure the animal behaves during its session.

Sometimes, the dog may fall asleep while the child reads. In that case, the owner might say, "Spot has closed his eyes so he can **concentrate** better on the story." If a dog is having a really bad day and becomes **anxious**, the owner may end the session early. Children usually are very understanding. After all, they've probably had a few bad days themselves!

If a dog falls asleep during a session, some owners may tell the child, "Congratulations! I often read to my dog at bedtime to get him to go to sleep. Now you've done the same trick with your good reading."

This yawning dog may soon fall asleep!

Everybody Wins!

Over the years, the R.E.A.D. program has been a great success. Most children who take part improve their reading skills. School test scores show they read faster, concentrate longer, and understand stories better. Dog owner Barbara Feldman explains, "When kids read to a dog, right away they start to relax, and pretty soon they enjoy the experience of reading instead of **dreading** it."

Kids aren't the only ones who enjoy the experience. The dogs seem to like it, too. They love listening to young readers and playing with them. Each dog offers love and attention, and the child offers love in return. That makes everyone feel "doggone" good!

Today, about 3,500 dogs take part in R.E.A.D. programs around the world.

Just the Facts

- Children in the R.E.A.D. program can bring their own books to read to a dog, or the dog's owner or handler will bring books for readers to choose from. Teachers make sure the books are right for each student's reading level—not too hard and not too easy.

- Students often read books about dogs or other animals. The books help the children learn about the ways animals behave and the right ways to care for pets.

- Teachers find that children who learn to read better usually become better students all around. School **attendance** improves because kids want to be in class more. They are also more careful about handing in homework. As a result, their grades improve.

R.E.A.D. DOGS

Shetland sheepdog

Golden retriever

Labrador retriever

Mastiff

Yorkshire terrier

anxious (ANGK-shuhss) afraid, nervous, or worried

attendance (uh-TEN-duhnss) the people present in a place

breeds (BREEDZ) particular kinds of dogs

canine (KAY-nine) a member of the dog family; another word for *dog*

commands (kuh-MANDZ) orders given to a person or animal

concentrate (KON-suhn-trayt) to focus one's thoughts and attention on something

confidence (KON-fuh-duhnss) a strong belief in one's own abilities

depressed (dih-PREST) very sad

dreading (DRED-ing) being very afraid of something

dyslexia (diss-LEK-see-uh) a learning problem that makes it difficult for a person to read or to understand what is being read

experiment (ek-SPER-uh-ment) a test set up to find the answer to a question

fleas (FLEEZ) small, wingless insects that live in an animal's fur and feed on its blood

handler (HAND-lur) a person who trains and works with an animal that performs a job

pronouncing (pruh-NOUN-sing) saying words correctly

qualify (KWAHL-uh-fye) to reach a level that makes a person or animal able to do a job

registered (REJ-uh-sturd) to be officially listed within an organization

residents (REZ-uh-duhntss) people who live in a particular place

restless (REST-liss) unable to keep still

session (SESH-uhn) a period of time used for an activity

specialists (SPESH-uh-lists) experts at particular jobs

stressful (STRESS-fuhl) full of tension or anxiety

therapy dog (THER-uh-pee DAWG) a dog that visits places such as hospitals to cheer up people and make them feel more comfortable

walkers (WAWK-urz) metal frames with four legs, used by people who have trouble walking on their own

Bibliography

Davis, Ronald D., and Eldon M. Braun. *The Gift of Dyslexia: Why Some of the Smartest People Can't Read and How They Can Learn.* New York: Perigee Books (2010).

Frei, David. *Angel on a Leash: Therapy Dogs and the Lives They Touch.* Irvine, CA: BowTie Press (2011).

Intermountain Therapy Animals, R.E.A.D. Program (www.therapyanimals.org/R.E.A.D.html)

Read More

Bozzo, Linda. *Therapy Dog Heroes (Amazing Working Dogs With American Humane).* Berkeley Heights, NJ: Bailey Books (2011).

Goldman, Marcia. *Lola Goes to Work: A Nine-to-Five Therapy Dog.* Berkeley, CA: Creston Books (2013).

Roberts, Jr., Walter. *Therapy Dogs (Dogs on the Job).* North Mankato, MN: Edge Books (2014).

Tagliaferro, Linda. *Therapy Dogs (Dog Heroes).* New York: Bearport (2005).

Learn More Online

Visit these Web sites to learn more about R.E.A.D. dogs:

www.angelpawstherapy.org

www.readtoroo.com

www.therapyanimals.org/R.E.A.D.html

Index

About the Author

Meish Goldish has written more than 200 books for children. His book *Disabled Dogs* was a Junior Library Guild Selection in 2013. He lives in Brooklyn, New York.